THE BLACK SHEEP IN MY FAMILY

Elizabeth Schooler is a mother of four children, three boys and one girl. She is an Evangelist and currently a member of the Lighthouse Seventh Day Christian Church in Bull Bay St Thomas, Jamaica. She is also a Motivator, a counselor, and a Philanthropist for three years. She was born on April 9, 1973, in the eastern side of Jamaica. She grew up in the humble community of Barking Lodge St Thomas. Her life struggles became her education, and Family, and friends. At the age of twelve, her dream to become a lawyer was put to silent. Because her foster parents withdraw her from secondary school, however, she allows nothing to stop her breakthrough; so, she pressed her way through with the help of God. Now she manages to start a non-profit organization called "Faith Motivation & Children Outreach

Foundation" that Assists the elderly and impoverished children throughout Jamaica. Plus, it did not stop there. "Risen from Abuse and Empowering Hurting Women Healing & Deliverance International Ministry" is her ministry as well. She endeavors to continue to reach out to women, men, and children nationwide.

Acknowledgment

First, I would like to thank God, the Almighty, for sparing my life and inspiring me to write this book. The journey from start to finish was not an easy one, but the Lord kept me through it all.

I would like to express my deepest sincere gratitude to my four children.

Raynardo Jones: the writer, my public relation officer

Shannoya Beezer: motivator, supporter

Rodcliff Jones: cover designer

Micheal Logan: my motivator, my supporter

Kassandra Carrasquillo: my motivator, my supporter

I also would like to offer my gratitude and appreciation to my Pastor, "Levi Rodney," the one who motivates and inspires me. Mr. Mark Evans, my best friend, my confidant, constantly pushing and saying yes, you can do it. Minister Michelle Evans, my prayer partner, motivator. She is also a member of both of my ministries. Also, I want to thank the viewers on Facebook; they encourage me to write and publish this book.

INTRODUCTION

For years I have been thinking about writing a book. I got several titles in my spirit from the Lord, but I decided to publish this one. The reason being a lot of people who are hiding share similar experiences with me without knowing it. I must thank the Lord again for His Inspirations to do this book, and I pray and trust God that it will inspire everyone that comes across it.

Are you familiar with the story of Joseph, Jacob's son in the Bible? Joseph had 11 brothers who were jealous of him. They sold him into Egypt and lied to their father about his whereabouts. While Joseph was young and living his life in Egypt, he faces multiple struggles, but he overcame them. "God was by his side:" fast forward, he became King over Egypt and helped his brothers and father during a famine. {Genesis 37-50 tells his entire life story}

My story is like Joseph but somewhat different. I was adopted at the age of 6 weeks old even though I had a family that could have cared for me. My mother had to make that decision whether to face confrontation or live-in humiliation.

Table of content

"How it Begin."

Open your imagination for a minute! Just Imagine a Shepherd having his sheep in labor. The sheep already has six lambs. The sheep's last lamb came out different from the rest. What would be your first reaction be?

My mother had seven children; I was the last one. My mother had an affair with another man, which is my father. Because I was from a different father, my siblings and mother treat me as an outcast, "the Black Sheep." After being six weeks old, my mother could not take the guilt anymore, so she decided to give me up for adaption/ find me a new mother. I am not even sure if she even thinks about it before her actions. I also believe her reputation plays a role in my adaption. She was a religious figure in her community and a spiritual leader. Well, the Bible tells us in Luke 15:4, "What man of you, having a hundred sheep, if he loses one of them, doth not leave the ninety and nine in the wilderness, and go after that which is lost until he finds it?". Did she come to seek after me?

In Barking Lodge, St. Thomas, Jamaica, my journey of being adapted has begun. At the age of seven years old, I realize something is wrong. My parents did not have any of my features; plus, their behavior towards me was different. I had two other siblings living with me, but it felt like all the hardship placed on me only. I remember I had to wash everyone's clothes by hand with no help from anyone. Can you imagine washing denim jeans, comforters, and thick women's dresses by hand? Oh, it was treacherous for a seven-year-old. Plus, they would only send me to school three days a week because I was their housemaid. The worst part if I refuse to do complete their work or use excuses such as I am tired, I will get thrashed. They withhold food, money, and anything that entertains a child. Evening though they provided shelter, food, sometimes, and clothes in my heart, I felt no Love. This Family I grew up with took advantage of my existence, worked me to the ground. The scars of my childhood scarred me physically, emotionally, and mentally.

By the age of 16, I grew tired of this treatment, so the opportunity presented itself to escape the dreadful lifestyle over 16 long years. Without looking back, I made a run for it, leaving my foster parents' home; it felt like redemption. This must have been what the slaves felt like on Emancipation Day. The rescue arms came from my young boyfriend, who became the father of my first three children. Well, that was slavery all over again, but we are not here to talk about that.

As the years pass by while living with my boyfriend, I was able to Mature and gain the guts to start the search for my biological parents. At 22 years old, I was equipped to take the journey to find my parents. So, I decided to start with my birth mother. If anyone were to be blamed or held accountable, it would be her. It is a mother's job to give tender love to a child she bears, so if I needed the truth, she would be the one to enlighten and reveal this mystery. Once I started to search, I was confronted by this friend from my childhood, and she told me that I bore a noticeable resemblance to a woman she had met before. I was thrown into a state of disbelief and uncertainty, but I decided that this would be a worthy gamble to answer my childhood questions with a leap of faith. In Hebrews 11:1, the Bible states, "Now faith is the substance of things hoped for, evidence of things not seen." I had to use this verse to encourage myself.

The journey continues. The level of suspense I was feeling was unbearable, having no idea who I was going to see. Even within that state, you could say I had butterflies in my stomach. I had important questions that were running through my mind. One of them was, "could this woman be my mother?" Next, what would she say to me? And what would I tell her? The thoughts decanted in from all directions, I even felt a bit timid, yet still, I pressed my way. What kept me going was the yearning to know the truth. The Bible states in the book of Saint John 8:32, "Then you will know the truth, and the truth will set you free." The only truth I was interested in was the reason why a mother would give up her daughter to strangers at the age of 6 weeks old?

After a long and quiet journey from my home community of Barking-Lodge, my friend and I arrived at the location that was supposedly my mother's home. While standing there, I examine the place to realize that the building in front of the yard was not structured like home. But a "revival church." This raised my suspicions, and the suspense got even more remarkable when I enter the church. My friend who accompanied me gave me specific instructions on how to approach my mom upon seeing her, "don't tell her who you are, and when she asks why you are here, tell her you are here for her services." Because I take up her advice, I had to carry the weight of keeping myself concealed. Now we are seated and waiting for my mom's recognition.

While waiting, I heard a woman voice saying "next person" outside the building. I was the next person in line to see her. I had to walk from the church to her house, which was next to the church. Her door turned, so I had to push it open. Once she saw my face, she smiled. Then what surprises me when she came out to the door to greet me. It had been like I have seen this lady before; it felt like déjà vu. It was all coming back to my remembrance. I had seen her face before in my dreams as a child. There was no essential meaning to the dream I was having. Now the lady in the dream from my childhood is the lady's spitting image standing before me. You can only imagine the state of shock I was in. It was like everything around me was frozen. She had on a head wrapped with a piece of cloth, and her skin was white. She was short, just me, and with only a glimpse. It felt like I was staring into a mirror. Without a doubt, in the world, I know this woman is my mother.

Now She turned around and looked directly at me, her FACE became exceedingly fierce, and my heart stopped beating. I was wondering what she would tell me? While she was looking at me, she just started up roaring into what seemed at the time to be the Holy Spirit. I was in disbelief, frightened, and do not know what to do. It seemed like my waiting had to go on a little longer. While standing in front of her, she started to give me messages from the Lord. One of them was how someone put their hands in my head and cause my hair to be pretty. Just pure foolishness if you ask me. So, my eyes were fixated on every movement, just waiting for her to acknowledge me as her daughter. But she did not!

Then she just called the next person, which was my friend. What a joke?

I was still there while she was reading up (like a psychic) my friend. She was telling her about her boyfriend and all that a woman would love to hear. Then the inevitable happened, my mother called me "Lady in the back." Then goose pimples filled my body as I walked to her. was this finally it (I wondered) was she going identify to the elephant in the room. She did not acknowledge the situation, maybe she was just as in the dark as I was, but I refused to believe that. In my thoughts, "as a mother, you could recognize your child and a person working for God, wouldn't He whisper it into your ear? Questions kept pouring in again, and I was there in my body, but my mind was far from my body.

Now she and I have a conversation; she asks me, "so, what you come here for today."

This was the chance I had waited for to unload, but I remembered my friend telling me not to reveal my identity. So, I answered "A read up," jokingly, just to see if she could connect the dots, but she never did. It seemed all she was telling me was going through one ear and going through the other. Such as I could have been wiser if my parents were not so poor, and someone cast a spell on my life to stop my progress. More like OBEAH. Nothing she was saying to me was sticking. I returned to my seat in the house, and what to seem almost half-hour ended in a split second. It was time to leave, and I had no concrete evidence she was my mother apart from resemblance and the smile she gave me.

I was back to square one. I was shattered at 22 years old. I felt neglected, a feeling of not being wanted. I felt a rush of emotions in my body as the tears came running as I stood alone. This journey had come to an end. The feeling of defeat ran through my mind, and my body shivered.

It was time to close this chapter on finding the woman that was my mother. My head hung down in shame and agony. A sense of not accomplishing what I set out for filled my atmosphere. Was this the end of all my hopes of finding the truth? All the time I put in became nothing but a wasted effort. I had to have faith Hebrews 11:6 stated that "But without faith, it is impossible to please Him, for he who comes to God must believe that He is and that He is a rewarder of those who diligently seek Him. So, I got up went home having faith that she would reach out to me, but that never happened.

Sometimes as Christians, we always expect things to go our way, but God is not "Santa Clause" he is a just God that works in our favor but not always to our liking but trust me when I say He has your best interest heart. A widespread encouragement I always give is that life is like an everyday journey. Driving on the road, you will never know what's around the next corner, but you still have to go around to get to your destination.

I hope so far; your hearts are being blessed because the journey continues.............

A MOTHER
AT LAST

Approximately three years after previously being let down; by my mother. The feeling of a heavy loss weighed on my life for those three years. From the moment I left that church with no concrete evidence that the lady was my mother. Throughout my days, the feeling of something missing continued to hover over my mind. Indeed, this could not be the end to my story concerning my Family.

The shepherd wasn't searching for the lost sheep, so with one last push, I made my mind up to go out and search again. What place could be better to start again, but with the lady who raised me, my adopted, the slave master? Seeing her again would revive memories about my life as a child, but I only got one goal in mind: finding my birth mom. So, I went to see my foster mother back in the community of Barking Lodge.

The memories flowed in like a bucket overflowing with water, but I persevered. All the domestic abuse from the past was coming back, but I had to overlook and put it behind me. I wasn't a Christian at the moment, so being unable to forgive her affected my mind. The Bible declares in Colossians 3: 13 Bear with each other and forgives one another if any of you has a grievance against someone. Forgive as the Lord forgave you. So as Christians now, we sometimes hold on to grievances, malice, and strife, but only a clean hand and a pure heart can see God. We have to put away all things that are not of God.

After meeting up with my adopted mom, I pleaded with her to accompany her to find my mother once more. I explained to her that I went to see a woman. She was the spitting image of me and told her about my experience at her church. Now she confesses that indeed I was her daughter. She recalled my mother's story giving me away as a baby to her to be raised and nurture.

My foster mother and I went back to the community where my friend accompanied me three years ago; it seemed deserted, but my hopes were still flying high. I wanted to confront her. Several questions passed through my mind, but I waited to see what the outcome would be. 'Motha" we shouted, but there was no answer. We called again only for a neighbor to answer "Motha nuh live deh so again," he shouted. You could just imagine the disappointment that came over me, but she wasn't dead, so there was still hope.

We went to the neighbor and interrogated him about the whereabouts of my mother. He quickly explained to me that my mom relocated to the community of Springfield. With a breath of fresh air, I sighed. But it was defeated. It was a delay, so we set out to Springfield. It was only a short walk up the road from where we were now, but the sun was boiling; frustration was not an option at this time—the bible states in Romans 5:4 perseverance, character, and character, hope. I want to elaborate on this scripture. Whenever we have a goal in mind that we aim for, "perseverance" is one of the main character strengths. Perseverance is the ability to never give up given the circumstances that are affecting your situation. Having the ability to persevere will develop your character, and character brings hope.

We arrived in the community of Springfield the search was on once more. Asking around, we got the proper directions to where is her new location. We came;

once again, it was another church-like structure. But it was what we call in those days a "shop church," just a building battened together to perform church duties. "Anyone Home," we called out; however, there was no answer, we called again, and a young man came out and inquired of us what the issue was. "Is mother home," I replied as calmly as possible; he too had a striking resemblance of my mother as well, so in the back of my head. I was saying this had to be my brother. He went and retrieved my mother, once again, face to face, my mother and me.

What could she say now? Was I standing there with my foster mom? Silenced filled the air for about 2 minutes no one wanted to speak first, then she broke her silence. "Then you are still alive," she asked my foster mom. That was all the confirmation I needed to know that she was my mother. But I said nothing; I just listened to my mother and adopted mother converse. I had to engage myself in the conversation promptly. I asked her why she did not tell me I was her daughter three years ago, she said to me that I should have returned when I spoke to me to, but how could I, what I wanted to hear three years ago, she didn't say it so why would I return.

She began to tell the story of my life before the sixth week. I am going to recall the story, but before I do, I want to pray with someone.

"Prayer for Perseverance and Endurance"

Our Father Who is in Heaven Lord I come before you, at this time to pray for this reader Lord. There is none like you Jesus, we could search the four corners of the Earth, and we still wouldn't find anyone like you Lord, we thank You for being who You are. We urge Your Holy Name. Father, your word is trustworthy and worthy of all praise.

Your comment is valid, and Your promises are faithful. When difficulties strike fear in their hearts, Lord, I know they can call on you for help. So, Lord, I stand in the gap for this reader. Whenever there is trouble, I pray You will be their shelter; whenever there is a fight, you will be their shield and buckler. Lord do for them as you did for David. Strengthen them like Elijah Lord, give them Courage as Samson. I pray for wisdom, knowledge, and understanding to rest upon their head. In Jesus' Name, I pray, oh Lord Amen.

.

A gloom came over my mother's face as she opened about my birth; I could see the fear that came over her body as she gazed while explaining the situation. She stated that it all began before my birth. She found she was pregnant, and it is by another man. Then she was alarmed, and fear gripped her heart. How could she keep it knowing her husband was abusive?

What a calamity, she brought back the memory of going into labor, passing out into a deep sleep; she recalled the angel of the Lord coming to her giving her with specific instructions "Don't give this child away," but she didn't take heed to the word. She went to the hospital to have the baby and fell into a deep sleep again; the angel visited her, saying, "Name the baby Elizabeth." She did just that but guess what? After I came into the world, five weeks passed, and the abuse intensified with her husband.

She would have threats from her husband to burn her house down, murder and kill her last child, which was me. After week six passed, my foster mother approached to collect the baby. With no hesitation, she did just that. What should I do with this information? Should I hate her, or should I love her? It seemed as if she had only good intentions, but why didn't she come back for me?

The abuse I went through could be compared to slavery while growing up. I heard the story, but how would I process it. The Bible teaches about forgiveness and how to exercise forgiveness, so I decided that forgiving her was the best way to approach the situation. I had to overlook 25 years of pain and hurt, a past that can be likened to slavery but guess what? We sin every day yet. Still, God forgives us and welcomes us into his grace with open arms. Romans 3:23 states that all have sinned and fall short of the glory of God. So, I decided right there that I would forgive her, move on and get to know the woman that gave birth to me.

LOSING

A

MOTHER

Meeting my mother was one of the best feelings, learning from her about her life and understanding what she went through; you can honestly say forgiveness helps calms the mind and gives peace to the heart. Learning from her widened my view of life. Honestly, this was what I lacked growing up. On the weekends, I would visit her to help clean up, cook, and sometimes even wash for her. Her stories always had me smiling and in awe; I hoped for this a long time ago; her stories went back before birth. She would often show me pictures of my siblings and how I resemble them.

One year later, the inevitable happened sickness struck her. She was trouble with serving high blood pressure; Nevertheless, I continued to visit her even more regularly than before. I always realized that I was the only child their majority of the time. What happened to the other six of her children? It was as if they didn't know she was sick? After a while, I was the only one visiting her and attending to her needs. I prayed for recovery, but it only got worse. After finally meeting my mother, she was fading away faster than the evening's sun. We tried everything together, both natural remedies and doctor-prescribed medicines, yet nothing made a difference. The light faded from her eyes as the days passed.

The fear of losing my mother gripped my heart. After all this searching, when I finally found her, she is being taken away by the cold arms of death. I braced myself for the impact of her death, made calls to everyone associated with her that I could get in contact with. Her sons took over from me and began to oversee her health. Eventually, they took her to the Princess

Margaret Hospital. I decided to cut back on my visits and prayed more often than usual. No one contacted me about her health condition. Days went by, and still, no contact. I reached out to her house phone number only to receive information that she passed. My heart tore it as if I knew her all my life, and she passed away.

Nevertheless, one year of connecting with her was enough to throw anyone into a state of depression. Thoughts began to run through my head once more, is it me, or does everyone leave my life eventually, first by neglect, now by death. Having no one to talk to, I sighed, left me alone with my thoughts—a terrible place to be.

"A Prayer for Depression"

Dear Heavenly Father, thank you that you never change, even when everything around me is changing and unpredictable. (Hebrews 13:8) Thank you that you are stable, even when I feel so very unstable. (Isaiah 33:6) It feels like Satan has been whipping me around! Please sustain me, protect me, and enable me to stand. (1 John 4:4; Psalm 28:7) I know that because sin entered the world, all creation is under a curse—all creation groans. (Romans 8:22) Because of this, I struggle physically, emotionally, and spiritually. Thank you for how my body is made and that it sends me warning signals to tell me that I need help. Right now, my brain and emotions are telling me that something isn't right. Help me to see if there is something physical that is causing my depression. Help me to sift through my circumstances to see if there is a need for change somehow. If I am experiencing depression because of a spiritual battle, please bring that to light and show me the best way to fight that battle.

Please lead me to the right source for help. Thank you for understanding what I am going through (Hebrews 4:15), and thank you that Your Word tells me that even Your Son went through hard times emotionally. There were times that He was distressed, grieved, faced loneliness, experienced deep sorrow, and after the death of John, He went into isolation (Matthew 14:13). He cried in prayer (Hebrews 5:7-9), and at times he was overwhelmingly sad (Isaiah 53:3). There was even a time that he was afraid his body would not survive the anguish he felt. (Matthew 26:38)

I pray that You would send someone to help bear my burden. (Galatians 6:2) Thank you for again reminding me of how weak I am and for the body of Christ that you have provided to help bear burdens when we grow too weary to bear them alone. I need someone to come alongside me, take my arms, wrap them around their neck, and help me walk until I am strong enough to walk independently. (Ecclesiastes 4:9) Thank you for the grace that you have provided. (Hebrews 4:16) I pray You will use this difficult time to cause me to go deeper in my relationship with You and that You would get the glory for anything that is produced in me. (James 1) Thank you for how you are going to use this time in my life and for all you are doing through this depression. Thank you that You have allowed my weakness to manifest itself in the form of depression so that You can work more of Your image into my life. (Galatians 2:20; Galatians 4:19) Thank you that I am not defined by this weakness. Since I am Your child, I am represented by what You accomplished on the cross. Because of Christ's death on the cross, I can wake up every morning and live life knowing that no matter what I do, think, say, or feel— the cross covers it. Because You offered up Your own beloved Son, I can have peace with You and can face each day with fresh hope and grace. Help me to focus on what is accurate and not focus on how I feel. As I sit before the cross, it helps me gain a new appreciation for what it means daily.

Help me to embrace my weakness as a gift. Remind me that my weakness allows You to work through me even when I am fragile and feel as though I can do nothing. (2 Corinthians 12:9) Through this time, I pray that you would enlarge my heart that I might love and obey You and love others more deeply. (Psalm 119:32; Galatians 6:2; 2 Corinthians 1:3-4)

Amen

Days passed; I finally found the strength to face my siblings. At that moment, I had my third child. I decided that I would attend my mother's wake just to show my respect. After arriving in the community of Springfield, I went to the house where we first met. The structure had memories pouring in from all over, so I entered the yard. Some of my siblings were seated. I recognized them based on the pictures I was shown. I was in awe when I saw how I closely resembled them. I got seated and tension-filled the atmosphere, eyes glared at me, and I was stared down. I felt as if I was under a microscope.

Persons who I didn't recognize were whispering. It was as if they had no respect that I was there. Suffering from neglect and low self-esteem, thoughts of feeling small and undermined began to pour in from all directions. Was it my babies that I had with me, or was it that I am still seen as the black sheep within the Family?

After being there for an approximate half-hour, I was approached by my brother. I felt even smaller, "we have decided it would be best if you leave," he said to me. I was escorted to the gate with my three kids. I had no idea what was taking place, and I was left in shock; it was clear that my 855rfamily had nothing to do with me. Feelings of neglect poured in once more, depression, resent everything terrible that you can think. Tears filled my face; the embarrassment I just experienced was just inhumane. After hunting down my biological Family, I was left out in the cold once more, A black sheep. That is all I am at this moment.

The Sunday came, and the funeral was set for 1 PM; I pondered on the intention of going, should I go and present myself to say goodbye to my mother. My mind halted on the opinion to pay my respects. After all, she did give birth to me. So, I got up, got dressed, and set out for the funeral.

Arriving at the funeral, the setting was somber; mourning filled the air, wails echoed. This must be the entire Family gathered. It took death for me to see all my Family. Her casket laid prostrate inside the church; I took my seat at the back while every Family sat at the front. The feeling of remorse filled my soul. I wish I had known her earlier, and I wish we could have had more mother-daughter time. The Pastor preached, he described her as a virtuous woman, a woman of no blame, yet here I was a secret affair. The funeral ended, and the graveside was the next stop. Again, a decision came to me to visit the graveside to see my mother for the last time or remain hidden. The courage came to me and the will to push on. So, I went to the graveside, the coffin was open, and my eyes caught sight of my mother for one last time.

The journey went through my mind, a year of reflection, the tears fell from my eyes. Without a doubt, we had established a connection over the year. Someone said, "Who are you to miss Gloria"? I looked up and dried the tears from my eyes. Then the person said, "What a girl fava Gloria" she screamed. The crowd took a turn soon, the attention turned to me, and everyone became curious, the Pastor proceeded with the graveside program, yet everyone stared at me.

Breaking the silence, I told the lady I am Ms. Gloria's daughter. She said to me, oh my, you are the baby my aunt gave away. She was alarmed and took me to other family members that I had never met and told them. They were shocked as well; it seemed to be my mother's secret was now in the open.

The black sheep was unveiled, spectacular timing, you would say. My brother's facial expression could be easily read, angry, disgusted, and ashamed that was the reading on their faces. The lady invited me back to my mother's home after the funeral to have dinner and talk. I was approached by a lady who was the spitting image of my mother. I've seen her in pictures, and I remember my mother telling me she was my sister. I smiled as she approached me, hoping it would've been a warm welcome to the Family; it was the complete opposite. "why had you had to introduce yourself at the funeral? Couldn't you wait". It was my time to be in shock, did I have any say in the matter, could I help to resemble someone who gave me away, my emotions were at the brim, and my smile retreated, but I said nothing. Her face had disgust written all over it. I felt

belittled by my older sister and guilty of a crime I were not involved in other than existing. I stayed for ten minutes and decided I wanted nothing to do with these people. They are instead be associated with barbarians than human beings.

Locking out someone guilty of nothing, I left with a dagger pierced heart.

CONCLUSION

Being a black sheep will always be a struggle we face together in humanity. Today I plead with society's families; do you have an outside daughter, son, cousin, or any family member that you treat as an outcast? I pray you today reach out and reconcile with that person or those persons. They may be wounded or left bitter because of the experience that they were born into. The scripture states that in first Corinthians 12:14-27; States

Even so, the body is not made up of one part but of many. Now, if the foot should say, "Because I am not a hand, I do not belong to the body," it would not for that reason stop being part of the body. And if the ear should say, "Because I am not an eye, I do not belong to the body," it would not for that reason stop being part of the body. If the whole body were an eye, where would the sense of hearing be? If the whole body were an ear, where would the sense of smell be? But God has placed the parts in the body, every one of them, just as he wanted them to be. If they were all one part, where would the body be? As it is, there are many parts, but one body. The eye cannot say to the hand, "I don't need you!" And the head cannot say to the feet, "I don't need you!"

On the contrary, those parts of the body that seem to be weaker are indispensable, and the parts that we think are less honorable we treat with special honor. And the unpresentable parts are treated with special modesty, while our presentable parts need no special treatment. But God has put the body together, giving tremendous honor to the factors that lacked it, so that there should be no division in the body, but that its parts should have equal concern for each other. If one part suffers, every part suffers with it; if one part is honored, every part rejoices with it.

We are all one in the sight of God. As the passage above states, whether we are the hand, head, or feet, we are still one, for the hand cannot function without the feet or the eyes without the ear. So today, if you take nothing away from my story, take this as a reminder; don't neglect a family member because of the life they live or where they stand in life. However, love them because by doing so, you are doing a good deed.

Ponder this, if you were born into a life of a black sheep, would you enjoy the feeling of being shut out or never included its rather distasteful to imagine that life. Today, if there is **Black sheep in your Family**, reach out to that person, stretch out a hand of acceptance, and reconcile with that sheep.

PRAYER FOR A BLACK SHEEP

Almighty God, I want to dedicate this prayer to everyone hurting from their experience of being an outcast in their Family; Father, please guide and protect them. Lead them in the right direction to help them to be successful but most of all, to give you their heart and serve you.

Amen

Made in the USA
Columbia, SC
27 May 2021

38641704R00033